T0146943

Endorsements

I absolutely love your collection of poems, Jen. They certainly stir the heart. They took me on a journey to my own childhood in Sydney with the horses and carts clopping up the street... I grew with you through the holiday times with a brother under the jetty and learning to swim, to the love of animals and the joy of flowering love. I wept at the loss of a beloved partner and parents. The only way to assess poems is from your own reaction and mine was heartfelt. Congratulations, Jen.

Margaret Kennedy, High School Friend
Armidale NSW Australia

These lovely poems by Jen Kimberley offer an intimate side of her that is honest and refreshing! Glimpses into these cherished moments of her childhood and history gave me pause to recall my own past with renewed life and vigor. I found myself remembering my father, family, pets, early days and relationships with a warm heart and even goose bumps. Each poem offers a colorful new look at experience and invites the reader to take a fresh look at their own. Thank you Jen for the courage it took to share these beautiful private moments with us!

Suzanne Hunt, Friend
Denver, Colorado USA

Poems
for Your
Heart

Jen Kimberley

BALBOA
PRESS
A DIVISION OF HAY HOUSE

This is a work of fiction. All of the characters, names, incidents,
organizations, and dialogue in this novel are either the products
of the author's imagination or are used fictitiously.

Balboa Press books may be ordered through booksellers or by contacting:

Balboa Press
A Division of Hay House
1663 Liberty Drive
Bloomington, IN 47403
www.balboapress.com
1 (877) 407-4847

Because of the dynamic nature of the Internet, any web addresses or
links contained in this book may have changed since publication and
may no longer be valid. The views expressed in this work are solely those
of the author and do not necessarily reflect the views of the publisher,
and the publisher hereby disclaims any responsibility for them.

The author of this book does not dispense medical advice or prescribe the use
of any technique as a form of treatment for physical, emotional, or medical
problems without the advice of a physician, either directly or indirectly. The
intent of the author is only to offer information of a general nature to help
you in your quest for emotional and spiritual well-being. In the event you use
any of the information in this book for yourself, which is your constitutional
right, the author and the publisher assume no responsibility for your actions.

Any people depicted in stock imagery provided by Thinkstock are
models, and such images are being used for illustrative purposes only.
Certain stock imagery © Thinkstock.

Print information available on the last page.

ISBN: 978-1-5043-8690-6 (sc)
ISBN: 978-1-5043-8691-3 (e)

Library of Congress Control Number: 2017913533

Balboa Press rev. date: 09/01/2017

Preface

Welcome to my portable poem world. Please dip in and out and feel free to post your comments at <u>www.jenkimberley.com/poems</u>. I'll be glad to respond.

Poems didn't begin coming to me until my second husband died in October, 1999. The grief loosened something and made or restored a creative opening. Though I've been paid to write technical manuals and websites, poems are unpaid and come from the heart. They have no business sense.

Some arrive intact, such as *A Small Mistake*, *Saturday Parade* and *When Widowed*, and receive no tweaking. But typically they arrive in a partially-formed state as described in *Poems* on pp. 86-7. They require that I put aside my novel, computer or kitchen task, grab a piece of paper, and start scribbling. Scribbling is a closer place to their entrance door than typing. They might arrive at 1 a.m. when I'm trying to sleep or any time when I'm home alone – ambient noise seems to intimidate them.

I believe that inside all of us, including extraverted party people, there is a private person who notices and feels much as I do. I think I'm typical, a standard specimen. We differ in how much attention we give to the private person. In all countries and eras, humans deal with the basics of love, death, sex, illness, family, work, success, failure and aging. Details vary and fashions come and go but these basics remain. It's up to each of us to deal with them in ways that are kind to ourselves and to each other.

I hope this small book speaks to you and feels like a friend.

Jen Kimberley
July 2017

Acknowledgments

My gratitude goes to my terrific son Dmitri George Kalmar who soaked up rays for a couple of days in a New York park while he read these poems and typed up his ideas and feedback.

Calligraphic border created by Freepik.

Contents

Green

With a wink to Kermit the Frog

Green is seeping back into our world
Replacing brown and gray—
Quiet and pale and hoping the snow
Won't be coming back our way.
No it's not easy being green
In a Colorado Spring,
And being yellow or blue or pink
Is not as simple as you might think,
When snow and wind can easily sink
And whisk away your work
And break and bend, undo, and send you
Back where you began.

But how many eons has Spring prevailed
While Winter raged his worst?
Winter can bluster and lay it on thick,
But a smile and persistence do the trick.

Jen Kimberley

The Angel

Late at night, empty streets dark,
My bike won't start.
I wheel it home, 4 or 5 miles,
Trying to keep my nurse's whites
Away from the grease,
Stopping at times to rest.

His note will be waiting
On the kitchen table:
"Dear Mummy, I did my homework
We ate the tuna caserole
We made a lego casle.
XXOO I love you".
Long eyelashes will be curving dark
On pink cheeks, his sturdy sword
(Garage sale bayonet from WWII)
Under his pillow,
Covers snug at his chin—

I walk on, debating what to say
At the teacher's conference next day
For my older son, stubbornly disdainful
Of school work, teacher's rules and demands,
He'd rather draw his hobbits and use those skillful hands.
Two more miles; my arms are tired;
I hear a sound behind and see
Another motorcycle pass;
Twice more it comes
And stops near me.

Backlit by the streetlight,
Black-clad, helmeted,
A stout silhouette looms tall and slow,
Reaching for my bike—

I clutch the handlebars;
He waves me away.
"What's wrong?" he growls
And hunkers down to poke around.
"Need a new part," he says as he stands.
"Can't do it now."

He rides away, and cycles around;
Passing me again each block,
Like a horror movie hound
Or giant bat from outer space
Circling a human speck.

He sees me safely to my gate,
Waves once,
And is gone.

Perspectives

We sat on the cantilevered, tree-shaded deck
    With cheese and mushroom omelets, toast and
    cups of tea,
Musing at the sand, astonishingly black,
Listening to the birdsong, the breeze and the sea.

His beard tickled my face as he leaned to kiss me,
His eyes beamed joy at the love he saw in mine;
The ocean rippled rushing tributes, bowing at our feet,
The sun peeped through the leaves and promised a day
    of his happiest shine.

From just a short distance along the rocky coast,
A hissing sound inserted itself into our tender dream
Repeatedly, directed by an unseen baton:
Giant drips of lava hitting waves and spurting steam.

Quiet and black above us with a secret red grin,
The primordial stream was creeping slowly down the slope
In partnership with gravity, encroaching on the green,
A trickle of death with power of unimaginable scope.

A few months later, we heard from a traveling friend
That the lava had taken a detour toward our secluded deck:
Our favorite Bed and Breakfast had come to a sudden end
In angry flames, and now was reduced to an undetectable
    speck.

Thus the island enlarges itself in its prehistoric way,
Destructive in the short term; geologically slow motion.
And those two lovers, cocooned in their own kind of heat,
Were transient creatures who drew a brief breath
On an incomplete mound of temporary ground
In a vast and ancient ocean.

Jen Kimberley

On a Sydney Beach

Scorching sun, pounding waves, children shouting,
Tanned, slim teens tossing beach balls,
Weary parents sunk in their siestas;
This teen listened, mouth salty, feet tingling,
Sore muscles soothed by warm yellow sand.

Once again she focused her restless mind:
Going to America with no plan to return;
Hoping to stay and marry her man;
Needing to grow and unlearn her shyness,
Become the woman she knew she could be:
That was the right choice, surely.

And you must remember,
She sternly imprinted on her own mind,
That later, if life over there becomes painful,
Too puzzling, or too hard uphill,
You must recall this day in the sun
When you knew it was something you had to do;
Adventure; a risk life demands of you.

She sat up again and gazed at the waves,
Rising, rolling, crashing, trailing;
Surely her soul could renew itself
Much like the surf; why not? She jumped up,
Grabbed her glide and ran to the water,
Splashed her way out for one final ride,
A Good-bye and Thank You to her sunny nation.

Ode to Music

We file onstage, wait for the moment
When the lights dim down,
And when there's no sound,
Our conductor strides in,
Nods his acknowledgement of eager applause,
Pauses, head bowed,
Gathering his focus.

Up come his arms, his baton gives the beat,
Two hundred ready singers rise to their feet,
And Music goes to work—
Trombones and trumpets make imperious announcements,
Flutes add their filigree, light and crystalline,
The harpist's hands are delicate,
The drummers stir the blood,
The violinists flash their bows
Busy in their pairs and rows,
And down with the basses, the cellos low and mellow
Give solidity and grounding to the sound.

Our singing is strong, though the work day's been long;
Latin words, or English, or German – never mind
What the language is, it's Music, it's wordless, harmonious,
It's universal love and the voice of humankind.

Jen Kimberley

We the Minority

It's odd being an introvert
In an extraverted world.
You listen a lot as you walk alone
And notice a lot that goes unremarked
By the busy, talkative, party folk
Who live on the phone,
Making things happen;
They keep the world spinning,
Dizzily so.

And who keeps it balanced?
Maybe its us:
The quiet amphibians, cruising below,
Rising at times to splash with the crowd
And check out the loud
And dramatic show.

Surely it seems there are two kinds of mind:
Things that for us might present an immense
Sort of challenge, like giving a talk,
Or entering into a loud crowded room—
Are as easy as breathing for party folk.

But catching the ironies, contradictions,
Noticing inter-personal play,
The canny and unacknowledged schemes,
Happens for us with no effort at all,

And we wonder anew every day
At all the obtuseness, so useless it seems.

We'll step up and speak and offer ideas
If it seems a good move—
But it suits us better to hold back and stay
Out of the fray,
Listening with one ear and tuning the other
Into a wordless universe.

Look West

In Denver the streets are a jungle, a tangle
Of cul-de-sac confusion, odd angles, roadwork,
One Way Only, obstructionist red lights—
Getting lost is easy.
But always in our sights
Are the mountains,
Which luckily are always in the west,
Their staff of angels keeping them resplendent in their
finery.
They orient the visitor, stop him getting ornery,
Raise us from the daily mess
To distant views and big ideas
And Nature's eternal scenery.

Woy Woy

A childhood paradise, Woy Woy was,
A calm cove near the coast—
No hotels, few shops,
Barely a road to our cottage.

Our Dad got us there in a black old jalopy
Up from Sydney at Christmas;
It jerked and croaked and bounced in the dust,
Sometimes stalled and tools were a must,
Till we broke through the gum trees and there it was:

Painted white; wraparound veranda
For sleeping secure in mosquito nets;
View of the water and run of grass
Where mushrooms volunteered.

There's our jetty, our rowing boat,
Twinkling blue behind;
Kookaburras cackle, seagulls soar,
And this child's heart grew huge.

Visitors came to occupy parents;
My brother and I ran off
With visiting kids for long hot days
Devising games in our endless ways
Under the shade of the jetty.

No weeds or mud – just clean warm sand,
Yellow and featuring crabs to chase—
We wondered how they hid so fast;
Fish further out near the jetty's end
To catch with string and an old bent pin
And wonder how they saw us coming.

I learned to swim at Woy Woy,
My Dad's hand under my chin;
I learned to love the salty air,
The rocking boat, the vaulted quiet.
Now my Dad has finally gone,
And my mother and brother and I'm alone,
And wherever I travel, my heart still loves
That vanished childhood paradise.

Young Argonauts

My brother and I played outdoors a lot
Our world was the back yard, the back lane, the park;
TV and iPhones not yet invented—
Only the radio; just before dark
It played a song in 6/8 time
Calling to children in Pied Piper style;
We dropped our games and raced inside
To listen again to Jason.

We were the Argonauts, manning his ship,
The Argo: a beautiful boat with oars,
And sails, and a purpose; our job was to row,
To help him find the Golden Fleece
And bring it to his home.

We had crew names; I was Ora 34.
Jason read our poems and stories every night.
Good rowing won a Blue, six Blues won a book.

Some days Orpheus came with his lyre,
And taught us songs; even our Mum
Sang along while she chopped and cooked.
He told of Hades' Underworld,
Of Cerberus and looking back and his lost Eurydice.

Phideas came too, to teach us how to draw.
He talked of the Parthenon, colors and lines,
Described our paintings, ideas we could use.
Hercules told of his twelve long labors:
Of Atlas, the Hydra and the dangerous Amazons;
He taught us how to eat well and grow up strong.

We grew up, we grew away: my brother's been a lawyer.
I became a fiddle player, student and disciple;
Teaching, singing, writing as I roam,
Searching for my Golden Fleece,
Rowing to my Home.

When Widowed

When widowed I shrank
　　To a thing of dry rustling,
A brown leaf rattling,
Cut loose and lost;
Caught in cross-currents,
Dusty, done, useless,
Debris wind-tossed.

We dashed around, aimless,
Rushed deserted byways,
Crackled in corners,
Paused, poised, to glance
Through warm yellow windows,
Recalling lost brightness,
And stop the dance,
Desultory delay;
Then back to barren blackness
And our gusty wayward way.

The months marched on, mathematical, neat,
Unmindful of my mindless arabesques.
And part of me plodded with unconscious feet
To the metronome's beat;
Keeping with the calendar:

Register the car now.
Pay the credit card.
Fix some food; ya gotta eat!
Sweep the messy yard.

Until somersaulting steadied,
And dimly I distinguished
The upwards from the down
And the forwards from the back.

And one night, a TV show
Made some sense,
Made me smile,
Caught my attention
And brought out a laugh.

I didn't know the sound.
No-one was around.
If he'd been there,
He'd have laughed too—
He always loved to share.

But now my task
Is to live and laugh
Without him.

Jen Kimberley

Glimpses Beyond

I came upon you in a dim, messy room,
Sprawled in a chair, long legs stretched out,
Looking bemused, and you let me know
That you had to stay there
Till the room was clean and bare,
A very large task, but one that you knew
You could do, if you could just
See where to start;
It was all Earth mess in which you'd played a part.
I woke in a sweat with a hammering heart.

You sat on the top of a soft grassy slope
With four other students, gazing out
At some celestial view,
Blocked from my sight;
And over to the side
Stood a dark-robed man, a Zen monk figure,
With a small knowing smile and a kind steady gaze:
The teacher. For a while he allowed me to stay,
But what he was teaching you, he wouldn't say:
He paused till I reluctantly drifted away.

One night you tenderly blocked my path;
You were made of shimmering gold,
You hugged me close and we shared our love,
And I tried to persuade you to stay;
But you had to leave for a far new place,
Where I wasn't able to follow
And you didn't know when we'd visit again;
And ever since then
The nights are hollow,
No longer deep,
Devoid of glory;
I simply sleep.

Jen Kimberley

In the Bookstore Coffee Shop

Six young women chatter and chirp
Sitting at that table; over here,
Teens are conspiring, collapsing in mirth;
Next to the window, discoursing quietly,
Two older men are quoting Christ.
I sit alone.

Memories jangle, jostle, prickle.
In those days we'd always share a table;
Tall as a crow's nest, he'd spy one somewhere,
And tuck his legs politely away
From unconscious customers bumbling by.
I brought the coffee with sugar and cream.
We browsed, studied, skimmed and conversed,
Caught up on favorite magazines.

At closing time we strolled to the door
Holding hands and gliding with us
A gold and blue aura, like sky over sea,
Curving around us, the space we created:
My love for him and his for me.

Bach's Presents

Bach is always with us:
Electrified, hooked on, re-arranged,
Jazzed up, ever adapted to the times.
Tinkling out of cell phones,
Warbling from alarm clocks,
Studied through the centuries, loved and revered;
Anna Magdalena still represents him,
Passing on his teaching to every neophyte.
As famous as the Danube in defining an age,
Rippling, singing, the brook forever flows;
Bach is always with us:
I wonder if he knows?

In German, "Bach" means "brook".

Seasonal Orchestra

A pair of flutes playing in thirds
Echoes the sound of springtime birds.
Mellow oboes and clarinets
Remind me of how hot summer gets.
Lamenting cellos can evoke
Fall's lengthening shadows and smell of smoke.
For winter's glittery icy spells,
I clearly hear percussion bells.

Jen Kimberley

Merri's Side of the Story

I called to you from inside my hedge—
You peered in the patios, the balconies, the treetops,
Poked around the parking lot, all around the edge;
You called out to me, but I had to hide,
And silently watched you give up the search
And retreat inside.

With the dark came big ice rocks
Hitting my hedge
And when they stopped,
I called you again.
Out you came, scanning under cars,
Standing a while in the cold to listen;
I crouched on the ground
Waiting to be found.

I waited through the second dark,
Feeling more weak,
Watched you load up the car next day
And drive away.
When you returned you brought a friend
And loaded up again—
Something then
Made me creep from my hedge
To be seen.

Warm hands scooped me up,
You exclaimed and petted, gave me water to drink,
The friend drove away, returned with bags
And a brightly colored box,
And while you piled up more in the car
I used that box
As I knew I should use it,
And nibbled some tasty chicken chunks
And hid behind the fridge
In warm dark seclusion.

So we moved together.
I crept up close and purred against your heart
To thank you and warm you in that lonely bed;
You cradled my skinny kitten frame
And fed me till my tummy was full and plump;
My long black fur grew glossy and clean
And my orange eyes regained their catly gleam.

So now I can prance and chase and stalk
Pink Mouse and all those strings you trail,
And sleep in the sun on the windowsill
Like a princess in a children's fairy tale.

On the night of the hailstorm, I was watching a documentary
about Lewis and Clark. It seemed to me that this little
cat was as brave in her own way as they were,
so I named her after Merriwether Lewis.

Jen Kimberley

Merri Makes a Friend

Who's that kitten you're keeping
Behind that closed door?
I know his smell pretty well now
And his pesky little meeow.
Well, that's better, let him out here
Where I can check him out.
Eeeeiow! Seeeya! aggressive little fella!
He'll have to come and find me
In this dark stairwell …

Hasn't anyone taught him manners?
He pokes his nose in where it doesn't belong,
Like into my bowl and my late-night snack,
Such a little egomaniac!
He jumps a lot, makes me lose
My concentration on the birds;
Crowds me up on my high cat platform;
I leave and find another place to snooze …

Today while you were out of the house
We had some chasing games;
He's such a runt, I always win,
I roll him over and chew his ears.
He's found the track ball and old Pink Mouse,
The spider dangling from the chair;
He crawls into every dark place he finds,
But I watch till he re-appears …

I'm keeping him cleaned up these days;
He can't keep up with himself.
I lick the dog slobber off his head,
And the dust bunnies off his paws;
Though he's getting a little bigger,
I can still enforce some laws,
And some days I even think
He's learning a few important things:
Now he knows his bed from mine
And hides with me when the doorbell rings …

Yes, I'd like a cuddle; feel free to scritch my head.
But what's that funny bumping sound?
That's Joe Bob batting his ball around.
Excuse me, I think I'll go and play
A game of soccer, and then maybe
He'll settle with me
On our cozy cat shelf,
Slip into a nap, perchance a dream
Of catnip and wrestling and bowls of cream.

Estrangement

I had a small brother,
My best childhood friend,
Who let me wash and comb his hair
And take him to the park,
And read to him at bedtime.
We played together on the floor
With blocks and bears and trains,
And I see us now, on the London street
Of sooty terraced houses in the soft grey rain—
A tow-haired little two-year-old,
Hands dangling at his sides,
Smaller and more lost
As his sister backs away, waving, slowly,
Till tears veil the view and she turns to run for school.

Back in Australia, we grew up in the sun,
A boy's world and a girl's world touching;
Till the girl became a woman
With a boyfriend in America—
Afraid to tell the news
Of her ocean liner berth,
Delaying, intending,
But a parent jumped in and told him in some other way.

Now we were strangers,
His blue eyes hurt: Why didn't she tell me?
He felt betrayed
And she didn't have the know-how to mend it.

The teen could not forgive me
For disappearing suddenly;
I came back for his wedding
But time had moved us far
And widened the oceans till planes were ineffective.
The young father died.
So the words were never said:
"I'm sorry, I apologize.
I love you very much;
Could we try to stay in touch?"

Jen Kimberley

Ode to Nuts

Almonds for a nut milk,
Pecans in a pie or
Pine nuts in a salad—
These are things to die for.

Walnuts baked in sourdough
With orange peel and poppy seeds—
Give your daily bread a boost,
Just what a hard-working vegan needs.

Nuts abound, they're all around;
They're just a tad retiring,
Hiding in a hard old shell—
But with some help
They'll respond quite well,
Pop right out, cast their spell,
And be culinarily inspiring.

Spice them up with a little salt,
Grind them up for a butter,
Chop them for a topping
On that special birthday cake.

And next time you're out shopping,
No need for you to stew on
What to buy; it's easy!
Create yourself a nutty life—
Something for people to chew on.

In the Museum

In the museum, years ago
She saw the El Greco alone on its wall,
A saint in the desert, eyes uplifted,
Praying devoutly, gladly in thrall
To his God, his hands clasped at his heart,
And around him dry rocks and pebbles and sand.

She sank to the bench, all else receding,
And something she didn't understand
Stole over her softly: intense concentration,
Joyful soaring of peace and content.

No sounds were around her, no people walked by,
No painting was hanging, no guards were intent
On surveillance, no husband was standing by waiting,
No body was breathing nor feet on the floor—

A saint was praying, or she was praying,
Or someone was praying – it mattered no more
Than which grain of sand was first caught by the wind;
Wind is, sand is, prayer is, and we,
If we paused to notice, would know ourselves safe
In God's gentle hands, in thrall and yet free.

Marriage Manual

—- For Noel and Casey McDonnell, September, 2007

Congratulations on your acquisition—
You've made a wise decision.
This ancient arrangement (though much maligned
By some who know little of how it succeeds)
Is perfect for those who love to love
And love to give
And know how to receive.

Remove it gently from its box
Of encrusted rules and rigid wrapping
(No need to recycle, just toss that away).

Step One: Examine it, being careful
To keep it safe from arrows of envy.
Insert in its center two long-lasting
Rechargeable batteries of patience and mirth.

Step Two: Adjust the Budget knob
To a setting of *Comfort* that pleases both users.

Step Three: At intervals, quite spontaneous,
Buy a surprise to insert in the slot
Labeled *Fun Refresher*.
It takes any gift that's original, seasonal,
Zany, extravagant, startling or reasonable;
Only make sure that it's made out of love.

Caution: Avoid all attempts at control,
As that will shrink the enthusiasm
Needed for longevity.
For maintenance, use communication
That's genuine, mutual, tactful and kind.

With sensible handling and daily care,
This marriage should last as long as you'd like,
As long as ye both shall share.

Jen Kimberley

The Maintenance Crew

In Denver the mountains are a backdrop.
God drew them very nicely with a fine tip pen,
And He colored them in
From the blue-grey end
Of His most subtle palette;
And when it was done, then

He hired a crew of angels, whose responsibility
Was to keep the paint from chipping as the eons roll on.
They formed themselves into
The blue team, the purple team,
Those who paint the winter white,
And those who paint the green.

Some days God drops a white veil of rain,
Or tosses out a misty shroud that hides the angels' work,
And the care they all took,
Coloring by the book,
But they tolerate His moods and just
Restore the layered look.

Some days, too, the mountain crew gets confused
With the sky crew, who are the masters of cloud,
From snarling black to whimsical white,
And preferring not to fight,
Collaborate in merging greys
And interweaving light.

Some might think this crew has a heavy workload;
They get no vacation time and working hours are long.
But they never dance on heads of pins
And they're exempt from singing hymns,
For doesn't painting honor God
Just as much as song?

Jen Kimberley

Pickwick's *Thank You*

She was black and wild, a feline refugee
From a world of dogs and trash cans and rain;
A shadow at the back door one Christmas night,
We welcomed her, pleased to ease her pain.

She accepted a snack and left for a week,
Reappeared one morning to request a little more;
And over the months she agreed to accept
Her meals atop the fridge by her familiar back door.

And over the years this straggly stranger,
Stepping in and out like a haughty aristocrat,
Made a home for herself on the fringes of our world,
Occasionally allowing us to give her a pat.

The trees behind our house became Pickwick's Woods.
She hunted and napped and patrolled her dominion.
And some days I'd turn to see, sitting neatly on the floor,
A feline statue watching me, withholding her opinion.

And one early morning when I put the kettle on,
I found beneath my chair, comfy, warm and dry,
A curled-up furry body in her final long nap:
A wild cat she was, but she came inside to die.

Ode to a Weed

Oh pushy plant, so stubborn, you persist in sprouting up
In the cracked old cement,
Trampled by children, chewed by the cat,
Hacked right down to a grinning green stub.

You re-sprout and unfurl your flowers, undaunted,
Lovely, large and lavender; but knowing that your time
Is sure to be short, you skip all the leaf stuff
And just bear the blooms, so pretty that I pick some
And arrange them as I'm able,
To grace the coffee table.

And I have time to do that because I'm unemployed;
Laid off, cut loose, hearing when I enquire:
You've done too many things, Ma'am, we feel you're
over-qualified;
We need a more exact match; the req was pulled;
we didn't hire.

So thank you, plucky plant, for teaching me to disregard
Discouragement, rejection; you show me how to thrive,
And continue to offer my humble summer bloom,
Regardless of reactions; and trust that I'll survive
Till someone plucks this handful
To grace a corporate cubicle.

Jen Kimberley

The Day We Met

My church sponsored a weekend
For motorcycle riders:
Thirty bikes roaring north
On Route One, leaning into
Innumerable curves, teetering over
Tall rocky cliffs,
Me a passive passenger
On my boyfriend's bike.

Early afternoon we pitched our tents,
Scattered to stroll through the forest
Or swim or gather driftwood along the beach.
But I was in the middle of a quarrel with that boyfriend
And it felt like one too many;
We weren't making any
Sort of headway, it seemed.

I turned away alone,
Stood near the trees.
And I listened to the voices
Receding –
The largeness of the place
Impeding any sound
But the soft little rustling, crackling, sighing
Of the forest, and the pounding of the sea
Muted by the dunes –
And my heart slipped free of its bond to the boyfriend
And rose up in hope
And lightness like the breeze.

I looked around with new sight:
The quiet empty clearing,
Picnic tables, benches,
Supplies stacked randomly,
All waiting in peace.
And off to one side the fireplace was set
Ready for the evening …

But what were those feet?
Two big sneakers resting on a rock,
Two long legs, two elegant hands
Clasped at his knees as he leaned
Slightly forward; two smiling eyes
Sending me a shy
And gentle
Greeting.

My heart moved again; I knew this man.
Yes, I'd seen him at the edges of the crowd,
Or strolling in late, helmet in his hand,
But aside from all that,
My heart knew this man
And it swelled up now
With a stillness, a fullness,
And my feet fell in line.
I walked over slowly and sat on the log
Beside him and we talked
Through the quiet afternoon.

Jen Kimberley

God had set that log out,
Upholstered it in velvet,
Shone His sun to warm our backs,
Sent His birds to sing along.
I learned about his young son,
His hard divorce, his army days;
His work as a computer network manager,
Foiling the hackers on the wild Berkeley campus;
A thoughtful man, a self-made man,
A clown and a gentle wit.

He lit the fire when the others returned,
And after we had feasted
People toasted their marshmallows.
I took my guitar and sang and took requests,

And everyone gathered
Around the lively flames
And sang along with me,
But in all that crowd, on that festive night,
I saw only one face:
I sang to love's light.

Love Song

I love you from a big place,
Hidden in my soul,
A still and steady wide place
Untouched by paltry mis-speaks,
By small mistakes, forgetfulness—
I love your laughing grace.

You take my hand when we walk along—
Your clasp is warm and affirming;
It draws from my heart a soaring song,
A hymn to this life that blesses us,
Sculpting our shapes with light-filled lines—
To you, my love, I belong.

Saturday Parade

In a coffee shop on a Saturday morning,
You can sit and watch humanity's parade:
Unrehearsed, expressive, unconsciously in costume,
The characters perform in Shakespearean charade.

Here's a young Dad with a small girl and a toddler,
He gently places chairs and his daughter's full cup;
Returning with his coffee, he finds a sticky mess
And an earnest little girl on her knees to clean it up.

Now a stout man, well-toasted by the sun,
Muscles bulging, long-haired, a modern Hercules;
He pours in the half-and-half, caps the cup contentedly,
And strolls out, his shorts flapping round his sturdy knees.

Here's a young girl wearing rhinestoned high heels,
Blond hair in abundance, completely black-clad;
She stirs in the sugar, no worries for the waistline,
And cocks her head coquettishly stepping past our Dad,

Who's cleaning up the second mess, a carpet of crumbs,
His toddler's face beaming as he tries to seize more scones.
And bubbling from a corner table, brimming with teens,
Come giggles and a babble and the shrill of cell phones.

Two gray-haired ladies, courteous and smiling,
Exchange their news of grandchildren, sip their herbal tea;
His coffee gone cold, a student's poking at his laptop,
Consulting books with academic equanimity.

Baseball cap shading his reflective sunglasses,
A man stands in line, arms folded, feet apart;
He grabs his two tall cups and strides out the door
Without a word or glance; perhaps he hides a hurting heart.

"Who's next?" floats over from the busy main counter;
"Coming right up!" "Nine-forty-eight please!"
Newspapers rustle, the radio warbles,
Sunbeams cross the floor by imperceptible degrees.

My car will be ready now; I gather up my things
And as I pass the Dad I hear him thank the café staff;
And mopping up the coffee mess he says to his daughter:
"Some days are like this; you just have to laugh".

Questions

Why not get a facelift
Or inject away this frown?
Why not up the cup size
For an elegant evening gown?

And where's my personal trainer
To help me flatten the abs,
Perform exhausting exercise
To melt away the flab?

Why not get my teeth straightened?
Certainly get them whitened?
Yet I can't help feeling chastened,
Dreaming up such plans.

I'm not like Liz or Shirley or Cher;
Success is not my face.
I ought to just be who I am
And try to age with grace.

Why is it that we worship youth,
When youth comes paired with ignorance?
What happened to respect for age,
And love for life experience?

Calling My Son

I so much want to call my son
And wish him Happy Birthday
And ask what he needs, what I could send;
I toss off my sweater, kick off my shoes,
Try to center and settle down,
Blink back the prickle, swallow the lump,
Get distracted, subside in a slump,
And days go by, busy as always.
Day after day, as his birthday approaches,
I tell my hand to pick up the phone;
I know he'll come when they call his name,
He's not alone;
He'll greet me and talk about movies or books,
And reminisce about people we've known
For several minutes before he's called
To Meds or Lunch, or he gets too tired
And must lie down,
And I'll wonder again, Was it something I did?
Or didn't do? Or didn't know?
A sensitive boy, so bright, so musical,
Healthy and stubborn – where did it start?
There must have been something I could have done …
I so much want to call my son.

Jen Kimberley

Open Door

My kitten tiptoes out the door
Cautiously sniffing and sensing.
Her orange eyes gleam in the April sunbeams,
Twitching ears catch the birdsong.
A V of honking shapes flaps across the sky;
Distant dogs are barking to and fro.
On the path beyond the fence noisy children run by.

Quietly she listens, sniffing the breeze.
Every moment brings a new sensation.
What a lot to learn! She never thinks to rush,
But holds still for maximum reception.

Squirrels, butterflies, raindrops and snow;
The grassy scenarios absent on a floor;
She doesn't yet know how much more
Her world will expand, but she's in on one secret:
The surprises you encounter, the richness of life
When you tiptoe through an open door.

For John, My Teacher

For John Fulton, Director of the Aesclepion Healing Center,
San Rafael, CA; RIP 2016

Somewhere there's a land of peace
Where the center holds together;
A WYSIWYG world, deception-free,
No password required, hacking unknown,
No-one needs an ID.

Simultaneously far and near—
Getting there, that's the trick.
Sometimes we stumble in during sleep;
Some music evokes it, or quiet reverie,
And we make an effortless leap.

But mostly the road seems impossibly steep
Or lost to our sight in a mist,
Or hostile with drop-offs or thorns or harsh stone;
Our progress seems backward as often as not
Or we're stymied by feeling alone.

We all need a teacher who knows how to laugh—
A guide who is certain and kind,
Who has been where we are and knows the way out,
Warns of the pitfalls, teaches us skills,
And dissipates fear and doubt:
Thank you, John.

Camouflage

Do moods and motives create our face?
Does the person we've been for all these years
Chisel and chip, twist and snip,
Paint our aging portrait?

No doubt; but there's more to the story.
Surely we have two kindly foes,
Two treacherous friends
Who help.

A cheering sun who greens the earth,
Coaxes crocuses,
Draws up daffodils,
Whispers encouragement to unfulfilled seeds.
His sub-plot slowly shows itself
When he toasts our willing faces
Till they match the wind-blown sand
And the dried-up Autumn weeds.

And our earth, that feeds and sings to us,
Grounding us to reality,
Who croons with the voice of honey bees,
Of mountain streams, of rustling trees,
Of crickets and birds and the cool night breeze—

She loves us and she wants us near,
Closer with every passing year.
We can't refuse; our bodies are hers
And little by piece they obey.

Our true self is hidden by our sun's handiwork,
Masked by our earth's possessive love;
But it's there for those
Who look to see
The spirit smiling through.

Jen Kimberley

Job Opening For an Angel

A silent, pale winter's day:
Even the bugs have abandoned us;
The passing planes sound extra loud
As they head for the Air Force base.
I cross the leafless, scrubby expanse,
Waning sunbeams wan on my face.
My dog bounds along, off his lead
And free to dash from scent to scent.

I walk to restore my optimism,
My faith and confidence,
Having failed again to be the one chosen
Out of the dozen or score or more
Of qualified applicants.

Is there a celestial employment agency
Matching up angels with jobs on Earth?
If so, I hereby notify them
That this human's hiring.

Wanted: a capable angel
To give good job search guidance,
Steer me towards appropriate openings;
Show me what I still need to learn
To climb from this wintry, jobless place,
Up into financial grace;
To whisper my name in each corporate ear
And restock my soul with hope and good cheer.

Hope

Gutters run, the eaves drip,
Autumn weeds are scratching holes
Through winter's clean white carpet,
A timid almost-springtime light
Is warming the bumps on skimpy twigs
With their promise of rose pink splendor.

My dog and I, we sniff the air,
He sniffs other things besides,
And I admire the blue lagoon
And picking up a pebble,
Toss it out to test the surface:
No, it's too soon.
It bounces, rattles, rolls away
And adds its shape and shadow
To the patterns on the ice.

There's no point trying twice.
We head for home, but though the sun's
Completing his decline,
It doesn't seem to be an omen,
Nor a harbinger
Of hard times still to come,
Of dark moods or loss of sight;
This time the night will soothe and comfort,
While we await the light.

Travel Plans

My love and I were cozy
In our sturdy old motorhome
Built to be owned
By a travel-loving couple
Who would tumble like two puppies
Around in its interior:
Nuzzle here, bump there,
Snuggle up on rainy nights
And dream of silent vastnesses
Of desertscape or sea.

He wanted me to see his land,
A native to an immigrant,
But first we parked where there were jobs
For our debt-abatement project;
Content to go on practice rides
On winding blinded side roads
Descending to the rocky coast;
Or flat and baking highways
Owned by overbearing trucks;
Through snowy white-out storms among
The grand Sierra peaks.

We made a plan for Baja
Where my love had watched the whales;
Another for the Rockies, where helped by his horse
He had dueled with teenage angst.
And two to see my grown-up boys...

But how can humans hope so high?
Our plans were suddenly dropped;
We stopped to study the hidden foe
Manning its black roadblock.

Together we took many roads,
In love to the last milestone,
Till we came to a way
Where I had to stay
And my love went on alone.

Jen Kimberley

Christmas

Whatever happened to Christmas?
It's been transmogrified
To solstice or winter or holidays—
Send out the cards: Happy Whatever!
String up the lights (but what do they mean?)
Listen to carols that sing about snowmen
And reindeer and sleigh rides
And bells—
And tell me again:
What's the connection?

What if we could agree
It's a day when we can pause
In our rush to make enough,
To afford a vacation
Or a bigger and a better
And a newer and a cooler …

But wait …
Christmas calls for thought, I think,
Some quiet contemplation;
A little admiration for a tiny new-born child;

And maybe just a moment
Of wonder for a story
That's been around two thousand years
And tells a truth to open ears
If only we knew how to quiet the chatter,
To stop and remember
To pause and ponder
The mystery
That is Christmas.

Jen Kimberley

In Defense of Mr. anyone

in response to ee cummings' *anyone lived in a pretty how town*,
which you can read at www.jenkimberley.com/poems

So anyone lived in his pretty how town,
And nobody loved him except his wife.
He reaped what he sowed and some children guessed
That really he didn't have much of a life.

Ladies and gentlemen, members of the jury:
The prosecution has made a strong case
That anyone lived like an unconscious weed,
Controlled by the seasons, in one provincial place.

I submit that this is a superficial view;
That much is omitted and much dismissed.
For one thing, anyone had a good marriage—
How many among us belong on that list?

anyone's town was peaceful and cared-for
And children could play without being afraid.
Singing and dancing were a part of life,
And church bells floated their Sunday refrain.

Isn't it true that the prosecution's beef
Is simply that anyone achieved no fame—
Never went to Hollywood; never wrote a book,
Went on TV or got public acclaim?

I ask you now: does this invalidate
His life of steady work and his loyalty
To his family and church and neighborhood?
Does it negate his reliability?

I submit that each of us has a life task,
A lesson to be learned, agreements to keep.
Our parents start us off by being who they are,
And the rest of life is follow-up, before we can Sleep.

Perhaps Mr. anyone had a full plate
Learning to be patient or humble or kind;
Perhaps in his previous lives on planet Earth,
He'd been a selfish hedonist with nothing on his mind

But hunting down his quarry to have his next affair.
Maybe he'd abandoned his children and his wife,
Or been a nasty punisher, or quarreled night and day.
So this time God said to live a peaceful life.

So I plead with you all, worthy members of the jury,
Not to forget, in your zealous haste,
That no-one is perfect; and what, really, do we know
That fits us to judge another person's life a waste?

Childhood Bedtime

With a nod to Wordsworth,
Intimations of Immortality

The small child looked forward to bedtime.
They turned off the light and shut the door,
Retreated to the living room,
Mother with her knitting, father with a book,
As they listened to Mozart and Bach.

She listened too, cozy in the dark,
Occasional car lights arcing across
The ceiling and leaving
The blackness as soft as it was before;
Crickets sustained their singing and chanting
Safely away in their world; in hers
Delicious peace seeped sweetly through:
Mysterious things were astir.

Lie still and focus, conjure up The Dot,
Watch that Dot, black spot in the darkness,
Think only of the Dot,
Until it happens:
The day drops away, the music recedes,
The Dot dissolves, leaving only a floatingness,

A oneness, a bigness,
A finished-ness in answer
To the question not yet posed,
But which later arose,
Of "Who exactly am I?"

In those early years, in the evening she remembered,
After long lonely days at confusing kindergarten;
Bedtime cleared the day's weary fog,
Restored the clouds of glory that children trail
    from God.

The Boss and His Deputy

In Denver the mountains are always on display.
God must have painted them centuries ago.
He used blue-grey for their default color,
And assigned to Father Time, who couldn't say no,
    As it's part of his job description,
        Temporal flow.

God was being forward-looking, as He tends to be
When He makes an acorn or a bank of malleable clay.
And He knew that in us He'd made a wayward beast,
Who'd want some entertainment and would tire of
    blue-grey,
    And He didn't want to bore us,
        Day after day.

Old Father Time is wise and knows how this will work.
Deep inside the mountains, unknown and unseen,
Is God's enormous database of colors and effects,
His array of commands; Father Time knows what they
    mean,
    And when he feels the urge, he chooses
        "Redraw the screen".

And a random combination of C, M, Y and K
Allows us lucky locals to be treated to a sight.
The brightness and the contrast are adjusted as we
    watch;
The hue and saturation, the shadows and the light;
    Technicolor is the mode — or some days
        Black and white.

October 10

Five years today it's been, since we lost him,
Yet the seasons still get their sequence right.
The sun hasn't noticed the vast black hole;
Rain falls unknowing through the long black night.

Small children laugh, unaware their tall friend
Has quietly withdrawn and softly moved on;
Cats still cavort and watch out their windows,
Unmindful that their loyal fan is gone.

Dogs are still playing and fetching their sticks,
Joyfully dropping them at the wrong feet.
Even the radio still plays his song,
Mindlessly grinding out its unheard beat.

One creature still grieves, though nobody sees:
My heart lives alone with its long memories.

Jen Kimberley

Tribute to Chopin

He belonged to no-one's school of playing,
Only his own, an original man.
He missed his family back in Poland
But Paris was home and he did his best,
As a highly honored guest,

Hoeing his loneliness into his music;
Sometimes a song with soft embroidery,
Delicate tracery in the left hand.
Wordless and haunting and healing our hearts
With tenderly intertwined parts.
Or a thousand butterflies flittering,
Flickering brightly, too rapid to catch;
Gliding, alighting at just the right moment,
Lingering, trembling, delighting the ear,
Transforming the atmosphere.

Some days his *angst* and outrage took over,
Storming the keys into wild ululations,
Loud undulations and fistfuls of chords
Crashing, protesting, pounding the bass:
A piano was too little space.
Or notes iridescently floating at leisure,
Like bubbles blown to enchant a child;
A glitter, a measured drip of silver
Or crystal: who hasn't been beguiled
By this sensitive man of uncertain health,
Who left us his musical wealth?

A Small Mistake

They say you should be careful what you ask for,
For that is likely what you will receive;
They say that what you live each day expecting
Is what will come about, with no reprieve.
I thought I sent the universe a clear plea
For what I'd like to be, and how, and when;
But instead of saying Prosperous,
I must have said Preposterous,
For here I am,
Laid off again.

First Encounter

He had named her Needles
And he loved her dearly
For her playful ways.

But someone in our busy house
Forgot to close the door.

Now she lies on the grass,
A fluffy grey heap.
My son creeps over to lean against my lap
Too shocked to weep.
I gather him up to cradle him close,
But Mommy's comfort is not what he needs;
It's Mommy's support while his life leads him
To this first encounter.

He maintains his gaze,
His young mind reaching
To penetrate the maze
Of God's hidden secrets,
And love's hidden cost.
We pay our silent homage
To a little life lost.

Unclaimed Parcels

I render unto Caesar what is Caesar's
And wonder how to render what is God's.
In a world so much in need of love,
Love turned down – that's the ache.
Perhaps this unclaimed parcel,
From its dusty back shelf,
Can send unwanted warmth
Out into the ether.

A hungry child in Africa
Might feel a subtle comfort;
A rioting adolescent might relent;
A prisoner in Siberia
Might be released.

And now I come to think of it,
There must be other parcels.
Perhaps there's one here in my house,
Sent to the previous owner.
Perhaps that's why at three a.m.
I feel at peace despite the ache—
Parcels are sent but when unclaimed
Are passed on to "any soldier".

Note: When you send a parcel to a soldier in a war zone, the
Post Office asks: What do we do if it's unclaimed? Return it?
No, you say. Check the box "Give to any soldier".

Jen Kimberley

Silent Sounds

We walk in this mellow brown and yellow world,
Winter's eerie silence creeping from the mountains;
Listen to the geese as they call to their stragglers,
And empty our sky.

The prairie dog sentries squeal at our approach,
Distant dogs bark, car tires swish,
Making white noise like a fringe around the park.

A nice walk, yes, but my heart is turned inward;
My ears hear what isn't here: the sounds of southern
    summer:
Yellow-crested cockatoos – a screeching flock of flowers
That alights and bursts each treetop into bloom;
Raucous unseen kookaburras
Flinging their opinions of these comic things called people
Waking up so late to merely stumble on the ground.

And thousands of cicadas with their own kind of ears,
For when you turn the Sousa march as loud as it will go,
And open all the windows,
They feel the vibration and their insect feet
Hum and thrum along with that eternal human beat.

The sound of green waves pounding the sand,
Blending with shouting and chasing in the water;
The call of a seagull wheeling and swooping:
Silent sounds from distant years,
A childhood in another era,
Half a world away.

Jen Kimberley

Long Ago Home

A humble house with a blue painted roof
And a shady front verandah—
A back yard of flowers and year-round green,
And an outhouse planted politely behind
Its criss-cross lattice screen.

In the house next door lived a shy young woman
And if she didn't see us peeping,
She'd play half the day on her festive banjo
Songs you'd want to dance to, and we knew the words—
We'd listened to them all on the radio.

Early each morning a horse clopped along
And stopped at our closed front gate.
A strong old man jumped down and lugged ice
To our shady back verandah where the icebox sat
Above the cockroaches, ants and mice.

"Old rags and bones! Old rags and bones!"
Another horse clopped by later,
Slowly, hopefully, and some days my mother
Ran with a sheet or a shirt she couldn't mend
Or pass from one child to another.

On Sundays a horse brought the children running out
As the ice cream man rang his bell.
We lined up with our threepences flashing in the sun
For our little tubs and spatulas, chocolate or vanilla—
For a while we were quiet and didn't run.

In winter came hail on the corrugated iron
Of our roof, making talk a pointless thing.
Our Dad lit a hurricane lamp against the gloom
Mum used the wood stove—the kitchen smelt good
And we camped out in that single warm room.

Christmas brought a sound that I heard from far away:
Trumpets, drums and flutes,
Slowly approaching till it neared our street
I ran out and followed the Salvation Army band
As they marched in the shimmering heat.

The house is demolished now; apartments fill the space,
The iceman pursues another trade;
Cars cram the street where horses used to please;
The pure silver threepences are now alloy cents,
And Christmas songs are mostly on CDs.

Jen Kimberley

Life Flow

Quiet and tiny,
Soft, sleepy, moist,
A baby at rest,
Gathering energy,
Listening, dreaming,
Abandoning its heavenly berth.

The small drop grows, turns into a trickle,
A glistening stream in a glade green from rain;
Moves slowly at first, as it ventures afield
From its hidden high cradle to rocky terrain.

Toddlers are frisky and pesky and joyous;
Movement feels marvelous, powerful and free.
Giggling, gurgling, play has priority:
Play is reality; learning to be.

Rocks to rush around, trees to ripple under,
Tumbling with the dappled shadows,
Mirroring the sky.
Meeting up with monsters but they burst like bright
    balloons;
Any clouds are white and fluffy, inviting you to fly.

One day it seems to suddenly be very different countryside.
Dark clouds frown.
Tall cliffs loom.
Obstacles are legion, causing frothing, foaming, worrying,
Stormy anxious questioning,
New desires, who am I?
And what am I supposed to do?

So it goes; the adult sighs,
And firmly treads from step to step.
Work to do, day by day,
Chores and errands, bills to pay.
Random rocks become more steady,
Form a bank, contain the flow;
Forward goes the rippling movement,
Spreading wide, becoming slow.

When the hazy blue horizon
Starts to croon a haunting tune,
What was once a sleepy trickle
Now is stately, tried and true.
Tests are over, tasks are done;
Lessons learned; we know our worth.
The harbor's arms are wide and warm,
And memory returns of that long ago birth.

My Violin

My violin's lost its singing voice,
It's hiding in its case.
It used to be a friend
With a sunny personality
Who came with me to parties,
Street fairs and concert halls,
Even to Church,
Singing loud and sweetly;
But now it sulks cantankerously,
Stares at me uncooperatively;
I think it needs some therapy
To help it cope with life.

Its voice is not entirely gone,
It's just gone all scratchy,
Gruff and reluctant.
Regardless of what music
I place up on the stand,
It doesn't like my hands.

As violins go it isn't old;
Its neck is firm and straight and strong,
Its bow can still move right along,
It still remembers perfect fifths,

But something in its stubborn soul
Has gone on strike; and so I hope
That somewhere there's a little girl
Whose mommy takes her out to hear
One of my violin's famous cousins
Doing some famous Beethoven singing,
And when they get home, their heads still ringing
She says with excitement: "Mom, let's begin!
I want to learn the violin!"

Jen Kimberley

Moving Along

The ocean liners are gone now;
Everyone travels by air.
Stuffed into their seat,
No room for their feet,
Having paid an exorbitant fare.

First the dash through the traffic,
Then waiting in line;
No bags unattended
Or there'll be a fine.
Then take off your shoes
And expect to lose
Your little ladies' Swiss army knife;
Give up your purse
Or things will be worse;
There's no time here for enjoying life.
The machine will squeal
With appalling zeal
At the wire in your bra,
But that's the deal;
There's no appeal;
Move along please,
Just wait your turn,
We're not here to ease
Your discomfort.

Once, as a child, I made an ocean journey
With my parents and brothers; the big ship waited
At Circular Quay, stately in her leisure, while
White-suited stewards trundled trolleys up the
     gangplanks.

All through the morning we milled around on deck,
Poked around our cabins, said our farewells,
Till ship's horn roared a warning; All Guests Disembark!
They struggled to smile through the last anxious hug,
Withdrew to the dock,
Our connections reduced to thin paper streamers,
A criss-cross confusion of colors, which broke

As slowly, the tugboats turned us around,
And the last thing we saw as they towed us out to sea,
Was my grandpa's black umbrella,
Waving small above the pack
"He's afraid," said my mother,
"He'll be gone when we come back."

From Sydney to London was six weeks' sailing,
Sea legs come easily for two girls running wild.
My new friend and I learned a lifelong love
Of warm wind and sea foam and phosphorescent fish.
We lived as free as the wheeling gulls
And the dolphins playing beside us;
The sailor in charge of stores gave us smiles
And all the treats we could wish.

Our ship raised parallel ripples in seas as smooth as glass,
Swished through the black and silver kingdom of the moon,
Detoured to the Cocos Islands, dropping off supplies,
Bucked through the gray and spray of tropical monsoons.

At night on C Deck stewards laid out cake and tea;
The band began, sent out the beat; my parents loved
    to dance.
Loners strolled the darkened decks; the swimming
    pool was full,
In shadowed corners couples kissed in shipboard romance.

Late at night I curled up in my cozy upper bunk,
Rocked like a baby, lulled by the sea's
Soft song at my porthole in its watery whispery voice;
The ship creaked a counterpoint so companionably.

Through the Great Australian Bight, from Perth up to
    Ceylon,
The Indian Ocean, Arabian Sea, the Red Sea, and then
The Suez Canal, at walking pace; sandy ancient pyramids;
Loaded camels plodding by with white-turbaned men.

Through the Mediterranean, around the coast of Portugal,
And so into the Channel till we came to ground again
In London's busy Tillbury.

The views from a plane are spectacular,
Their speed of ocean transit is impressive, we know;

And the pilot of a small plane flies free with the birds,
Using levers and buttons instead of air flow.
And giant cruise ships now pack in their passengers
And steam around in circles
Expensively.

But the world has lost a treasure,
And we have lost the pleasure
Of those old ocean liners
And that gracious life at sea.

Jen Kimberley

My Dad

A half a world away he lives alone
Under a summer sun at Christmas time,
Still making jokes and taking walks each day,
Talking like a man still in his prime;
Reading just as much as he always has,
And still enjoying concerts, films and plays;
Learning how to surf the internet,
In no way at a loss to fill his days—
A man like this is always in the sun:
No-one can believe he's ninety-one.

Rough Seas

For seven years the seas have been rough—
My solitary boat has bobbed and bucked,
Splashed into hollows, climbed the slopes,
While I bailed and rowed and held onto ropes,
While heartless storms blew black and brusque,
Across our invisible path.

I did have a route in mind to steer,
And a compass of sorts, though it couldn't be seen,
Deep as it is in my stubborn soul,
But its needle was faithful through pitch and roll,
My star remained true through each blank night
And winked to lift up my heart.

The storms did their worst and slowly withdrew,
Sending a wild-mannered cousin or two,
Hoping to sink us, but giving up
In the face of tenaciousness, ever more tough;
For that was the outcome – my boat held strong
We stayed together, moved right along,
And my soul is still singing its song.

A Life Divided

White flakes clutter the air
Quarreling over which way to hurry
Whirling, backtracking,
Evidently reaching eventual agreement
That things low are where to go.
Their silent siblings chase behind,
Orphaned output of some celestial
Population explosion
Beyond our blanked-out view.
They crowd each other, fighting for space,
Slump and lie like little bodies
Heaped in mass graves
On path, shed,
Garden bed.

My heart pines for a coastline,
Shimmering now through long summer days;
A green-blue sea capped with pleasantly scattered
White flecks; a far clear horizon
With maybe a couple
Of slowly progressing pointed white specks;
For yellow sand like a warm welcome mat,
Dotted with brightly colored umbrellas;

For shouting children chasing, splashing;
The satisfying thud and sizzle of surf.

But close white silence surrounds me now;
I live a life divided.

Kindergarten Kids

Earth is a kindergarten where we learn the basics;
We're little ones starting to walk.
Don't hit Johnny – he'll hit you back;
Don't throw sand – you'll get it in your own eyes.

"Do unto others …" is a hard one to follow
When we feel so certain that we're right and they're wrong,
And we think that being right entitles us to judge,
Forgetting that the other guy is certain he's right.

Why is it so hard to forget and forgive?
What a rare accomplishment to Live and Let Live.

Planting a Nation

With a wink to England.

More than two hundred years ago
In London Town upon the Thames
The English had a problem that
Resisted all their stratagems:

Prisons were too full of felons—
Even creaky makeshift jails
Made from rotting boats that squatted,
Stuck in mud and stripped of sails—

Until they got the bright idea
Of bundling these embarrassments,
Along with many half-trained soldiers
Rousted from the tenements

Together in a vessel that was
Strong enough to stay afloat
Until it reached the antipodes,
Safely distant, thankfully remote.

And so the prison problem was solved.
But far from the fog of Britannia,
Unknown to the judges who stayed behind,
A sunburned country was beaming a smile

At its ragged new residents laden with chains
As they shuffled around at work in the quarries,
Building the barracks, the roads and the drains,
Their hopes so low and their hearts full of worries.

For though both convicts and settlers feared
To hear the cocky kookaburras
Cackling loudly at private jokes,
And scarcely could contain their horror,

That deadly ants and bugs and spiders
And snakes were always underfoot,
And grass was yellow instead of green,
Distances vast, the sun too hot;

And though it seemed impossible
That Christmas was in summertime,
And nowhere was the North Star seen,
Yet these tough and canny limeys

Found that time was on their side;
That fine sheep fleeces were guaranteed,
Found that when they ploughed and planted
Wheat, it grew exuberantly.

Jen Kimberley

And who needs bluebells who has the waratah,
Or holly when there's the Christmas bush?
What use are stoats or moles or voles
When kangaroos abound, and the platypus?

And so the love began to grow
For this strange land that seemed able to nourish
The convicts' dreams and the settlers' hopes,
And babies were born and a new nation flourished.

Night Time Oasis

In her childhood's chilly desert
There was an oasis.
She circled around
And found it at night
When the lights were off
And the door was shut.
The heat flowed up
Like a wave at the beach,
A rush and a flush of debris disappearing
Till her head was hot
And her body relaxed
And the healing hum
Mended all the gashes
Where the axes had landed that day.

With her pieces reconnected
And her strength restored,
She rested in a bubble of peace.
Bedtime was the best time
Of every childhood day,
Though she never knew the name:
Kundalini.

Jen Kimberley

The Pollster

The election season flushes him out
From under his enchanted rock
To stir a numbers brew.

He digs out his dog-eared recipe book,
Unpacks the occult abacus,
And his cloak of royal blue.

First the agenda must be promoted:
He reads the memo sent out that day,
His guide, whether false or true.

Aligning his brewing pot to match,
He ponders the stock ingredients,
The foundation of his stew.

A scrumptious scandal, a myth, some leaks,
Some innuendo and luscious lies,
A ruined career or two.

Decide on a margin of error for safety,
One eye on next season's credibility—
That, he'll never eschew.

And finally add a generous sprinkle
Of hot and piquant statistical seasoning—
Now for the interview.

We see him smiling and being polite,
Exuding authority, sketching out
Somebody's Waterloo.

Then his eyebrows beetle, his fingers twitch,
With a flick of his cloak he begins to preach:
"Mirabile dictu—

"No need to bother with counting votes;
You'll find the truth is in my poll,
Everyone trusts my cool voodoo!"

Jen Kimberley

The Other World

The creek is still slow and trees are still bare
But mild winds blow and Spring's in the air.

My dog and I, we swing along,
Away from the crowds and under the roads.
Beyond the pond and wild apple groves
To another world that nobody knows.

The trail divides; we take the other track,
Over the hill where the tall grass grows;
Listen now! Do you hear the call
Of the Bellbird, guiding us on where to go?

When all noise is gone and the world becomes still
We come to a glade of dappled shade;
We sprawl out comfortably on the grass
Near the ducks and swans on the pond.

Our Bellbird retires to keep watch in a tree;
Friendly magpies flock to say hello;
Talkative, playful, some swing upside down
Beak firmly fixed to the willow's dangling fronds.

Little lizards visit us with news of their friends;
Bees take a break to bring us the buzz,
Dainty little ladybirds rest on our hair
And whisper loving stories of the flowers.

Leprechauns live here and hobbits and elves
With prairie dogs the guardians and geese the air patrol.
No humans are allowed unless they have an escort
With four legs, a good nose, and friendship true and whole.

Poems

Poems lurch up from the vasty deep:
The disorganized unconscious mind,
The basement where we tend to keep
Messy heaps that we never sweep,
And endless miles of untidy piles
of things unfiled.

They lug along some words and a general idea,
And a feeling that goes with it and a rhythm to be used,
And maybe also bring some tears,
And memories from forgotten years,
And useless fluff, and other stuff
in an old duffel.

Their hair unkempt and their shoes unlaced,
They land with a thud on the mind's front porch.
They stare at your astonished face,
And challenge you to start the race
Before they stall, walk into a wall
or stumble and fall.

You empty out the duffel then and look at what they've
brought,
Hoping you will have some time without an interruption,
You might be re-enacting an old war fought,
And you know that the puzzle will take some thought,
And you pray that you can stay
to see the way.

Then you patch and you stitch and you paste and
    re-arrange;
You comb and you iron and cajole them to cooperate.
At first their new appearance may seem rather strange;
You persist because you know that it is within their range
    To stay here, get clear
        and captivate the ear.

When at last they stand and face you, sturdy on their feet,
With all their various parts and different facets
    resurrected,
And they're clean and have a shine, you can lean back in
    your seat,
And admire this new creature, and be grateful for the heat,
    And the stir and the mirth
        Of a worthy sort of birth.

About the Author

Jen Kimberley came to America in 1963 on a student visa to do a Master's degree in music. Since her only job skill at that time was typing, which she had taught herself before she left Sydney, she supported herself with a series of typing jobs using those machines that we now see only in antique shops. In 1968 she married and subsequently had two sons. Over the years she has lived in both Australia and America and is now a dual citizen.

Her first published book was *A Child's Guide to Sydney*, the first such guide in Sydney, in 1977.

In 2001 in Denver, CO, she was diagnosed with Chronic Myeloid Leukemia and her second published book was *My Cancer Survival Saga And How You Could Star in Yours* (October 2016). In a novel-like style, it tells her cancer story: how she obediently took the official pill for eight years and then realized that it would never cure her; how she tried two alternative protocols by herself without knowing enough and almost died; and how she was taken by her son to a cancer clinic that saved her.

It covers the alternative treatments she received between 2012 and 2014, describing them both subjectively as they felt to her and objectively in sidebars. Addressed to cancer patients and their loved ones, the Saga lays out an organized approach to steering your own cancer care with chapters on diet, questions for your chemo doctor, helpful non-IV treatments available to the public, cancer causation theories and much else. Upon publication, marketing and publicizing were withheld from this book because it covers alternative cancer treatments. However it is available at www.jenkimberley.com and at the usual online booksellers.

In September 2016, Kimberley moved from Australia to Illinois to be near her older son. She has continued her alternative cancer self-care, living nearly six years now past the date when AMA statistics decree her demise. At the time of this writing the leukemia appears to be fully cured. Her next book will describe how she finally achieved that.

The poems in this current book have been written in the years since Kimberley's second husband died. The grief somehow triggered them and some are poignant; but many are light-hearted or amusing, and they cover a wide variety of subjects.

Printed in the United States
By Bookmasters